Contents

Introduction

Here are a dozen little interactive books to help students explore the theme of neighborhood and community. Each book provides students with both a story to read and an activity to try as they learn about the people and places found in different living environments.

The books cover a range of topics—from goods and services to transportation to community helpers to urban versus rural living, and more—that will help students develop an understanding of what neighborhoods and communities are and how they function. You can use all of the books in sequence to build a complete unit on the theme of neighborhood and community or pick and choose among them to enhance your existing curriculum.

The mini-books are easy to make and easy to use. You'll find instructions for assembling the books on page 5. Teaching notes for completing the activity in each mini-book and extending the lesson are included on pages 6–26.

Students will cut, paste, color, draw, write, and even manipulate a cut-out character as they complete each mini-book activity. As children read each story, they'll expand their vocabulary, practice decoding text using picture cues, and deepen reading comprehension. They'll also gain practice in using a variety of other skills, including sequencing, map reading, adding math facts, using money, and critical and creative thinking.

In addition to reading the books in class, encourage children to take their mini-books home to share with family members. These experiences give children valuable reading practice and further strengthen their confidence as readers. A comments section is provided on the back cover of each book where family members can provide positive feedback about their child's developing reading, writing, and thinking skills.

Enjoy your trip around the neighborhood!

SCHOLASTIC

Reading-for-Meaning Mini-Books

Neighborhood and Community

By Maria Fleming

NEW YORK • TORONTO • LONDON • AUCKLAND • SYDNEY
MEXICO CITY • NEW DELHI • HONG KONG • BUENOS AIRES

Teaching *Resources*

Cover and interior artwork by Anne Kennedy
Cover design by Maria Lilja
Interior design by Sydney Wright

ISBN: 0-439-10433-5

Copyright © 2005 by Maria Fleming
Published by Scholastic Inc.
Printed in the U.S.A.
2 3 4 5 6 7 8 9 10   40   12 11 10 09 08 07 06 05

How to Make the Mini-Books

The steps children take to complete each activity are different for each mini-book. These steps are explained in detail in the teaching notes section (see pages 6–26). To assemble the actual books follow the directions below. Instructions for assembling the book "Here Come the Firefighters!" vary slightly, however. To make this book, follow the instructions provided on page 16.

Demonstrate for children how to create one of the books, going slowly over each step. Then guide the class through the steps again as they complete their own individual mini-book. Of course, depending on students' age and skill-level, you may want to assemble the books yourself before class and distribute the ready-made books to students.

You'll want to have scissors, glue sticks, and crayons on hand for students to complete the activities in each book.

1. Copy the pages for books on standard 8½- by 11-inch paper, making the pages single-sided.

2. Fold the front cover/back cover in half along the dashed line, keeping the fold to the left side.

3. Fold each inner page in half, keeping the fold to the right side.

4. Place the inner pages inside the cover and staple three times along the spine.

Welcome to My Neighborhood!

(Pages 27–30)

About the Mini-Book

What better place to begin an exploration of neighborhoods and communities than in students' own backyards! In this mini-book, children will draw pictures of some of the people and places they see every day.

Making the Mini-Book

1. Duplicate and pass out pages 27–30.
2. Help children assemble the books by following the general directions provided on page 5.
3. Invite children to draw pictures of their neighborhood to go with the text on each page of the book.
4. On page 6 of their mini-book, help children write sentences describing what they like best about their neighborhood.

Teaching Tip

Allow time for students to present their books to classmates and talk about the details they included in their books. What do their neighborhoods have in common? How are their neighborhoods different? As a class, develop a definition of what a neighborhood is—for example, "Neighborhoods are places where people, live, work, and play."

Taking It Further

Take a Walk Encourage students to pay closer attention to their surroundings by taking them on a neighborhood scavenger hunt. Create a list of specific things that children should try to find. For example:

> something shiny,
> something red,
> something tall,
> something furry,
> something loud,
> something with wheels,
> something with writing on it,
> and so on.

Provide each child with a copy of the list. Include space for students to record their observations, then take a walk around your school neighborhood. Children can compare their observations back in class. You may want to make extra copies of the list for students to take home so they can undertake the scavenger hunt with a family member in their own neighborhood.

I Like Living in the City

(Pages 31–34)

I Like Living in the Country

(Pages 35–39)

About the Mini-Book

Not every community is the same. In these two mini-books, students will get a glimpse of the sights, sounds, smells, and tastes of two distinctly different living environments: urban and rural. Because this activity involves several multi-step parts, you may want to tackle it over the course of several days.

Making the Mini-Book

1. Provide each child with two envelopes. Have children label one envelope "City Life" and one envelope "Country Life."

2. Duplicate and pass out the cut-and-paste page on page 39 and have students cut the sentence strips apart.

3. Read each sentence strip aloud. After reading each sentence, ask children to decide whether it describes life in the city or life in the country and to place the strip in the appropriate envelope.

4. To complete the mini-book "I Like Living in the City," duplicate and pass out pages 31–34.

5. Help children make the books by following the general directions provided on page 5.

6. Have children review the contents of their "City Life" envelopes and decide which sentence strip matches the picture on each page of the mini-book. They can then paste the sentences in place.

7. To complete the mini-book "I Like Living in the Country," provide children with copies of pages 35–38 and repeat steps 5 and 6 above, using the sentence strips in the "Country Life" envelope. (The completed pages, with sentences in place, are shown on page 8.)

I Like Living in the City

I like living in the city.

I like to see the tall buildings that touch the sky.

1

I like to hear the noisy music of cars and taxis honking down the streets.

2

I like the yummy smells coming from all the different restaurants.

3

I like to taste the salty pretzels that vendors sell on every corner.

4

I like to feel the rush of air on my skin when a train goes thundering by.

5

I like living in the city. There's nowhere else I'd rather be!

6

I Like Living in the Country

I like living in the country.

I like to see the rolling green fields that stretch for miles.

1

I like to hear the sound of horses galloping through the pasture.

2

I like the fresh smell of hay that's just been cut.

3

I like to taste the sweet, crisp apples from our neighbor's orchard.

4

I like the tickly feel of a sheep's wooly coat.

5

I like living in the country. There's nowhere else I'd rather be!

6

Continued

Teaching Tips

* After reading both mini-books, encourage students to talk about which setting they would prefer to live in and why. What do they like about each setting? What do they dislike?

* Point out to students that a third type of neighborhood, known as a suburban neighborhood, has things in common with both city and country neighborhoods. Allow time for children to compare and contrast their own neighborhoods—be they urban, suburban, or rural—with those described in the mini-books. Be sure students understand that there is great variety among neighborhoods, even within each of these categories.

Taking It Further

A Sense of Place Create two charts on separate pieces of posterboard. Label one chart "City Life" and the other "Country Life." Divide each chart into five labeled columns, one for each of the senses: see, hear, smell, touch, and taste. Make an extra copy of the cut-and-paste page with the sentence strips on it. Enlist students' help in sorting the strips according to the environment they describe and the sense they correspond to, and then have them paste the strips at the tops of the appropriate columns. Encourage children to come up with as many additional sights, sounds, smells, etc., as they can for both country and city environments. Add their contributions to the appropriate columns of the chart.

Sensory Walk Students can sharpen their observational skills by going on a sensory walk in the school neighborhood. Have children bring their journals and encourage them to use all their senses as they record their findings: What colors do they see? What sounds do they hear? What are some of the textures of the items they find in the school environment? Tastes and smells might be more difficult to identify, but encourage children to include them if possible. (For example, if there is a pizzeria in the neighborhood, students can imagine what the pizza would taste like.) Create a class big book that chronicles some of the sights, sounds, tastes, and smells of your school neighborhood. Students can try the same activity at home to create sensory portraits of their own neighborhoods.

NOTE: Before taking your walk, review safety rules with students, reminding them that they are not to touch any sharp or otherwise potentially dangerous objects and that they are not to put anything in their mouths.

Busy, Busy Saturday

(Pages 40–45)

About the Mini-Book

What goods and services do communities provide? Where can these goods and services be found? Students will explore the answers to these questions as they follow a boy and his father on their Saturday morning errands around town.

Making the Mini-Book

1. Duplicate and pass out pages 40–44.

2. Help children make the books by following the general directions provided on page 5.

3. Distribute copies of the cut-and-paste page on page 45 and have children color and cut out the neighborhood places. Review the name of each location with students.

4. Each page of the mini-book describes an errand a boy and his father must complete. Students should find the picture of the neighborhood location where the two would go to complete the task and paste it in place on the page.

5. On the line provided on each page, children should write the name of the location they pasted in place. (The completed pages are shown on page 11.)

Teaching Tips

* Point out to students that this story highlights a variety of places found in a *community*—a group of neighborhoods.

* The parent and child in this story live in a town where they can walk from place to place to do their errands. Invite children to share their own experiences running errands with family members. Where do children and their families go in their community to get the things they need? Is everything in one place, like a mall or downtown area, or are things more spread out? What form of transportation do children's families use to complete their errands?

Taking It Further

Location Lotto Provide children with magazines and ask them to cut out pictures of different buildings and places found in communities. Talk about how these places meet residents' needs in some way—for example, for work, school, worship, recreation, and so on. For each building or location, have students identify what activity takes place there by completing this sentence frame:

This is where people go to _____
_____ .

Then write each sentence on a blank index card. Glue each picture on a separate blank index card. Label each picture. Mix the cards up and have children use them in a game of lotto, matching each place with the activity performed there.

Make a Model Create a quick and easy model community using brown paper lunch bags and grocery bags. Brainstorm a list of buildings and places that communities should include in order to meet their residents' needs. Randomly assign each child a building (such as a post office, bank, hospital, house, or apartment building) or place (such as a park, airport, or zoo). Then have students draw the building or location on a bag. Open the bags to make them stand, and enlist students' help in arranging them to make your model community. You may want to use strips of masking tape to represent streets in the community. Students can use dolls or finger puppets and/or toy vehicles to show residents and workers going about the business of community life.

The Library

(Pages 46–50)

About the Mini-Book

In this mini-book, students accompany a young girl as she visits her favorite neighborhood place—the library—and help her add up all the books she checks out during the course of a week.

Making the Mini-Book

1. Duplicate and pass out pages 46–50.
2. Help children make the books by following the general directions on page 5.
3. Point out the math problems in the dialogue balloon over the bookworm's head on pages 4–7 of the mini-book. Tell children to write the answer to each problem on the line provided. (The completed pages are shown on page 13.)

Teaching Tip

After children have solved each addition problem, show them how they can check their answers by looking at the problem on the next page. The sum of each problem will be the first number in the equation that follows it. Children can also count the books in the pictures to help them solve the addition problems and to check their answers.

Taking It Further

Favorite Places In addition to providing for residents' basic needs, every neighborhood and community has something special about it. Provide each child with a piece of drawing paper that is approximately 6 1/2 by 9 inches. Ask students to draw pictures of their favorite place in their immediate neighborhood or larger community. Mount students' drawings on pieces of colored construction paper that are 8 1/2 by 11 inches. Use the pictures to create a class quilt of favorite neighborhood or community places. Allow time for children to talk about their pictures and why the building or other place they've depicted is their favorite neighborhood spot.

Neighborhood Math A study of neighborhood and community life abounds with opportunities for integrating math lessons. Here are some more ideas to try with students:

★ Estimate the number of sidewalk squares on a given block or the number of houses or buildings on a block, then go for a walk and count them.

★ Be a stoop snoop. Sit on the steps or look out the window of a school, home, or shop and count the number of cars or people who pass by in a 15-minute period (best in the city, where there's a lot of street activity). Compare the pedestrian or vehicular traffic outside different places.

★ Go for a neighborhood shape-walk. Find all the circles, squares, rectangles, and/or triangles you can during a neighborhood walk.

★ Compare the sizes of different buildings on your block or in your community—for example, from tall, taller, to tallest or from small, smaller, to smallest.

Who Helps?

(Pages 51–55)

About the Mini-Book

In this mini-book, students will get to know some of the workers we depend upon every day to keep our communities clean and safe and running smoothly.

Making the Mini-Book

1. Duplicate and pass out pages 51–54.
2. Help children make the books by following the general directions provided on page 5.
3. Distribute copies of the cut-and-paste page on page 55. Have children cut out the dialogue balloons. Each dialogue balloon includes a simple description of the job a particular community helper performs.
4. As you read each page of the book, ask children to find the dialogue balloon that describes what that worker does and paste it in the space provided. (The completed pages are shown on page 15.)
5. On page 6 of the mini-book, invite children to draw a picture of another community worker and write the name of the worker on the line provided. Help children compose a simple sentence describing this worker's job and write it in the speech balloon.

Teaching Tip

Ask students to identify some of the community helpers whom they rely upon every day. First, suggest that they make a list of their daily activities—for example, waking up, getting dressed, eating breakfast, going to school, and so on. What community workers make it possible for them to complete these tasks? For example, farmers grow the food they eat each day, truck drivers bring the food to market, store clerks sell the food, and so on.

Taking It Further

Mystery Helpers As a class, generate a list of community helpers, including those named in the mini-book. Write the name of each community helper on a slip of paper. Students can take turns picking slips of paper from a hat and pantomiming the actions their chosen worker might perform on the job. Classmates try to guess the worker's identity. Use the list of helpers on page 15 to get you started.

Community Helpers

baker
barber
bus driver
construction worker
crossing guard
dentist
doctor
farmer
garbage collector
grocery store clerk
librarian
mail carrier
mechanic
newspaper carrier
nurse
paramedic
restaurant chef
school teacher
shoe repair person
telephone repair person
train conductor
truck driver
veterinarian

All in a Day's Work Students see many community helpers at work every day in their very own school: teachers, secretaries, cafeteria workers, custodians, crossing guards, bus drivers, and so on. During the course of a week, invite a different school worker to your classroom each day to speak about his or her job. Help children prepare questions before each presentation. At the end of the week, students can create special cards for the workers they met, thanking them for their contributions to the school.

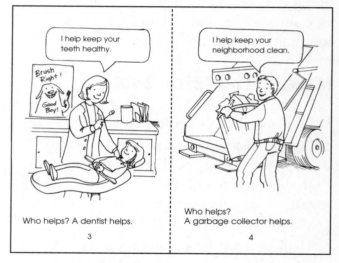

Here Come the Firefighters!

Here Come the Firefighters!

(Pages 56–59)

About the Mini-Book

In this mini-book, students will take a closer look at the specialized job of one group of community helpers: firefighters.

Making the Mini-Book

1. Duplicate and pass out pages 56–59.

2. Instead of folding the pages to make the book, students should cut along the dotted lines to separate each individual page. The pages are out of sequence and do not include page numbers.

3. Help students decide the proper order that the pages should be in to tell the story. They can then number the pages from 1 to 6 in the blank box provided at the bottom of each page.

4. Once they have verified that the page sequence is correct, students can staple the pages together along the left edge to complete the book. (The completed pages, in sequence, are shown on page 17.)

Teaching Tip

Before reading the story, ask children to describe what they think happens at a fire station when a call comes in that there is a fire. As children offer their ideas, write them on chart paper or the chalkboard, using words like first, next, then, and last. Keep this sequence of events posted for students to use as a guide as they assemble their mini-books.

Taking It Further

Meet the Firefighters Arrange a class visit to a local fire station so that students can see the gear and equipment firefighters use in their jobs and hear firsthand accounts about life in the fire house and the dangerous and exciting job of fighting fires. If a class trip isn't practical, help children generate a list of questions about the work firefighters do and compose a letter to send to the nearest fire station.

Play It Safe Part of being a responsible community member involves following safety rules to protect oneself and others from harm. Divide the class into small groups and have them brainstorm a list of safety rules that it is important to follow—at home, in their schools, and in their communities. Each group can then pick one safety tip to highlight on a poster. Children can hang the posters around the school and in other community locations as public service announcements.

A call comes in.
Ding! Ding! Ding!

1

Slide down the pole
as the bell starts to ring.

2

Put your helmet on your head
and boots on your feet.

3

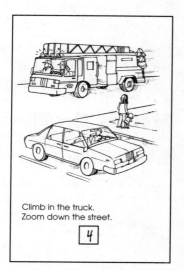

Climb in the truck.
Zoom down the street.

4

Raise the ladder, higher, higher!
Aim the hoses at the fire.

5

Everyone is safe
and the fire is out!
"Hooray for the firefighters!"
the people all shout.

6

The Mango Man

(Pages 60–64)

About the Mini-Book

Some community workers provide services and some provide goods. In this story, students will use play coins to "purchase" some of the colorful and delicious goods a neighborhood fruit vendor has to offer.

Making the Mini-Book

1. Duplicate and pass out pages 60–63.
2. Help children make the books by following the general directions provided on page 5.
3. Distribute the cut-and-paste page on page 64 and have children cut out the coins. Talk about what each coin is worth and compare their different features—for example, the front and back of each coin, the historical figure pictured, and their relative sizes. Younger students may want to write the value on the back of each coin as a reminder.
4. On pages 2–6 of the mini-book, students should select coins to equal the price of the fruit pictured and paste the coins in the box provided. Tell students that they do not have to paste coins in all of the boxes on each page.

Teaching Tips

* There should be enough room in the box at the bottom of each page to paste the coins. However, if students choose to tally the total of each purchase using some pennies—and as a result have more coins than will fit in the box—they can paste those coins on the back of the page.

* Remind students that there are different ways of combining coins to equal a given price. After students complete the activity, invite volunteers to share the combination of coins they pasted in their mini-books to equal the price of each piece of fruit. You may want to list all the different possible coin combinations for each item on a chart. (Completed pages, showing sample coin combinations, are shown on page 19.)

Taking It Further

★ ★ ★ ★ ★ ★ ★ ★ ★ ★ ★ ★ ★ ★ ★ ★ ★ ★ ★

Let's Go Shopping Bring in sales circulars and invite each student to cut out three items that he or she would like to buy. Each item should cost no more than $1–$1.50. Students can then paste each picture on an unlined index card and write the cost of the item beneath the picture. Make extra copies of the coin patterns on the cut-and-paste page and distribute them to students. What combination of coins would students use to pay the exact amount for each item? Students can paste the coins totaling this amount on the back of each card.

Fruit for Sale What would students like to buy from the Mango Man? Children can set up their own make-believe Mango Man Fruit Stand to both dramatize the story and gain hands-on practice using money. Ask each child to bring in one or two pieces of fruit from home. Arrange the fruit on a table in baskets or bowls. Have children decide on the price of each kind of fruit and make signs listing the prices. Use a cardboard box to make a cash register and set out bags for purchases. Students can use play money to make transactions, taking turns assuming the roles of customers and sales clerk.

The Mango Man sells fruit to everyone in town.

1

He sells an apple to Mr. Alvarez,

2

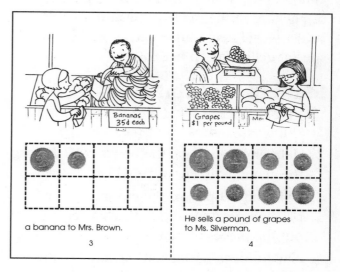

a banana to Mrs. Brown.

3

He sells a pound of grapes to Ms. Silverman,

4

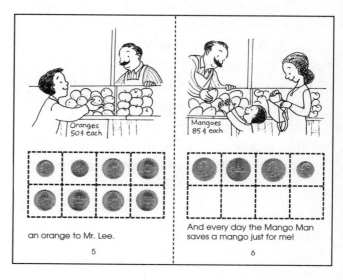

an orange to Mr. Lee.

5

And every day the Mango Man saves a mango just for me!

6

The Mail Carrier

(Pages 65–69)

About the Mini-Book

Who doesn't love getting a surprise letter or package in the mail? In this mini-book, students will help a mail carrier make some special deliveries on her route.

Making the Mini-Book

1. Duplicate and pass out pages 65–68.
2. Help children make the books by following the general directions provided on page 5.
3. Distribute copies of the cut-and-paste page on page 69 and have children cut out the pieces of mail.
4. Children should look at the address on each piece of mail, match it up with the corresponding house in the story, and paste the letter in the box provided at the top of each page.
5. Have students write their own address on the package at the bottom of the cut-and-paste page. They can then paste the package in the empty box on page 6 of the mini-book. (The completed pages are shown on page 21.)

Teaching Tips

* Before reading the mini-book, show students a few pieces of mail and review the different parts of a person's address. Then have students flip through the pages of the mini-book. Direct their attention to both the street sign next to each house in the story and the number on the front of each house. Show students how they can determine the street address for each house by putting these two elements together. Then direct students' attention to the pieces of mail on the cut-and-paste page and ask them to point out the street address on each one.

* After reading the story, ask students what "surprises" they've received in the mail. Invite them to share their experiences. What's their favorite kind of mail to get?

Taking It Further

★ ★ ★ ★ ★ ★ ★ ★ ★ ★ ★ ★ ★ ★ ★ ★ ★ ★ ★

Mail Call Set up a mail center in your classroom and give children practice writing, addressing, and "mailing" their own letters. Students will enjoy making their own play stamps to lick and stick. Display a variety of postage stamps and examine the pictures on each. Then invite students to design their own stamps. Create "glue" for the stamps by stirring together 2 tablespoons of flavored gelatin mix with four tablespoons of boiling water. Show students how to use a paintbrush to apply the "glue" to the back of the stamps they designed. After the stamps dry, students can lick or wet the backs of the stamps and stick them onto envelopes.

Stamp Stars Point out to students that many stamps honor people and the contributions they have made to our nation and our world. Can students think of people in their community that they would like to honor with a stamp? Their stamps could celebrate school or community helpers, good neighbors, or other individuals who enrich their community in some way. Create an oversized stamp template on a standard-sized piece of paper. Include several lines for writing beneath the stamp. Provide each child with a copy of the template. Have each student draw a picture of a community helper he or she would like to honor. Help children compose sentences that explain why they chose the community member they did. Students may then want to mail their stamps to the people they celebrate.

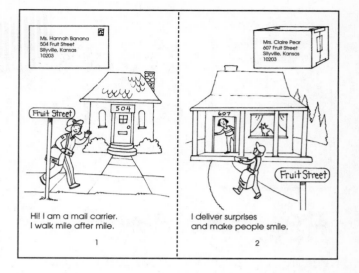

1   Hi! I am a mail carrier. I walk mile after mile.

2   I deliver surprises and make people smile.

3   I deliver cards and letters to people every day.

4   I bring packages and postcards from people far away.

5   I like being a mail carrier. It's an important job to do.

6   Maybe one day soon I'll bring a surprise addressed to you!

Trucks Come and Go

(Pages 70–76)

About the Mini-Book

People depend upon various forms of transportation to get around and to move goods from place to place. This mini-book highlights a form of transportation that is often a source of fascination for young children: trucks.

Making the Mini-Book

1. Duplicate and pass out pages 70–75.
2. Help children make the books by following the general directions provided on page 5.
3. Distribute copies of the cut-and-paste page on page 76 and have children cut out the trucks.
4. On each page of the mini-book, children should paste the picture of the truck that the text describes. (The completed pages are shown on page 23.)

Teaching Tips

* This book features trucks that people might see in a city neighborhood. What kinds of trucks might students see in a rural area? What kinds of trucks do students see in their own communities?

* Point out to students that some trucks do things (cement mixers, snow plows, back hoes, and so on), while other trucks carry things (delivery trucks, moving vans, ambulances, etc.). Reread the book and have students classify the trucks according to these two functions. Can they think of other trucks that belong in each category?

* Talk about other vehicles we depend upon. How do students get around their neighborhoods? What other types of transportation are found in different communities?

Taking It Further

Big Wheels What kind of truck would students most like to drive? Invite them to draw pictures of their favorite trucks, putting themselves in the driver's seat. Children can complete this sentence frame to include beneath their pictures:

I'd like to drive a _____ because _____.

Bind the pages together to make a class book about trucks.

Graph It Make a graph that shows which trucks are students' favorites. Use information on the graph to create word problems for students to solve. For example, "How many more people like bulldozers better than dump trucks?" Help students express each problem as a numerical equation before solving it.

In my neighborhood, trucks come and go.

1

Some trucks move cars.

tow truck

2

Some trucks move furniture.

moving van

7

Some trucks clean the street.

street sweeper

8

Some trucks move snow.

snow plow

3

Some trucks mix cement.

cement mixer

4

But my favorite truck of all

9

brings a sweet treat to eat!

ice-cream truck

10

Some trucks dig dirt.

back hoe

5

Some trucks help people who are sick or hurt.

ambulance

6

Lost!
======

(Pages 77–82)

About the Mini-Book

This mini-book introduces students to maps and gives them practice following simple directions as they help a lost dog find its way home.

Making the Mini-Book

1. Duplicate and pass out pages 77–81.

2. Help children make the books by following the general directions provided on page 5.

3. Distribute copies of the cut-and-paste page on page 82. Have children color and cut out patterns A and B.

4. Have children fold the two-sided dog character (pattern B) in half along the solid line and glue the two halves together.

5. Direct children to glue pattern A in place on the cover of the mini-book. They should glue only the bottom and sides of the pattern  to the cover, leaving the top edge open to create a pocket. (When students have pattern A in place, it should look like the dog character is sitting in his dog house.)

6. As you read aloud the text on each page, ask students to move the dog character along the streets, turning where the text says to turn. (See page 25 for Noodle's location on each two-page spread of the book.)

7. When students have finished reading the story, they can tuck the dog character inside the front cover pocket for safekeeping.

Teaching Tip

For older students, you may want to draw a compass rose on each map inside the mini-book. You can then make the directions a bit more challenging by prompting students to move the dog character north, south, east, and west along the streets named in the story.

Taking It Further

Make a Classroom Map Tell students that maps provide "a bird's eye view" of a given area—that is, they show what an area might look like to a bird flying over it. Ask students to imagine that they are birds flying over your classroom. What would they see if they looked down? Provide students with drawing paper and help them create simple classroom maps.

Giving Directions Pages 3–4, 5–6, and 7–8 of the mini-book all contain maps. Cover the text on these pages of the mini-book using correction fluid or by other means. Make additional photocopies of one or more of these maps and distribute them to students. Choose two locations on the map (for example, the library and the fire station on pages 3–4) and ask children to trace a route from one building to the other. Have children write or dictate directions between the buildings, based on the route they traced. Point out to students that there are different ways of getting to the same place, and that maps can help us choose the shortest or most convenient route.

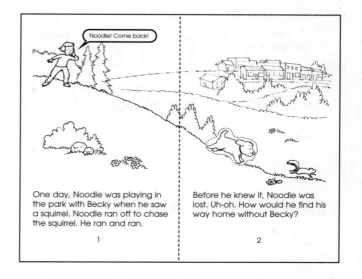

One day, Noodle was playing in the park with Becky when he saw a squirrel. Noodle ran off to chase the squirrel. He ran and ran.

1

Before he knew it, Noodle was lost. Uh-oh. How would he find his way home without Becky?

2

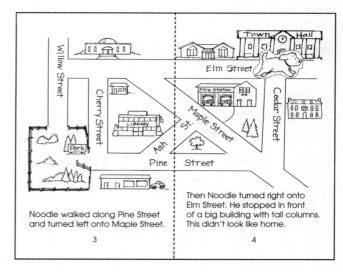

Noodle walked along Pine Street and turned left onto Maple Street.

3

Then Noodle turned right onto Elm Street. He stopped in front of a big building with tall columns. This didn't look like home.

4

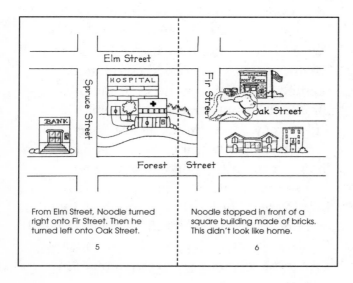

From Elm Street, Noodle turned right onto Fir Street. Then he turned left onto Oak Street.

5

Noodle stopped in front of a square building made of bricks. This didn't look like home.

6

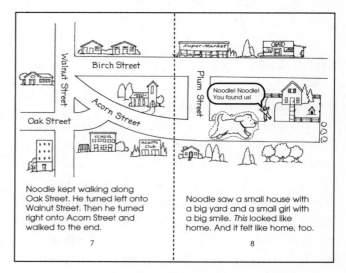

Noodle kept walking along Oak Street. He turned left onto Walnut Street. Then he turned right onto Acorn Street and walked to the end.

7

Noodle saw a small house with a big yard and a small girl with a big smile. *This* looked like home. And it felt like home, too.

8

25

Dream Neighborhood

(Pages 83–86)

About the Mini-Book

This mini-book describes an imaginary neighborhood that includes a number of silly and surprising features.

Making the Mini-Book

1. Duplicate and pass out pages 83–86.
2. Help children make the books by following the general directions provided on page 5.
3. Invite children to draw pictures on each page to go with the descriptions of the fantasy neighborhood.
4. On page 6 of the mini-book, tell children to circle whether they "would" or "would not" like to live in the neighborhood the book describes, and help them write a sentence that tells why or why not.

Teaching Tip

Point out that although the neighborhood this book describes may sound silly and fun, it still provides for some of the basic needs of the people who live in it. Ask children to identify which of these needs the neighborhood meets (for example, homes to live in, transportation, places to play and attend school). What problems might living in this neighborhood present—for example, if all the stores are toy stores, where do people shop for food, clothing, and other goods?

Taking It Further

Dream On Ask students what features they would include in the neighborhood of *their* dreams. Provide each child with an oversized piece of paper and have him or her complete this sentence frame:

I'd like to live in a neighborhood where

_____.

Ask students to draw pictures to accompany their sentences, then bind the pages together to make a big book entitled "Our Dream Neighborhood."

Neighborhood Caretakers We can't all reside in the neighborhood of our dreams, but we can work to make our neighborhoods better places to live. Discuss with students what it means to be a good community member. In what ways do they and their families act as neighborhood caretakers? (They may, for example, recycle their garbage, help a neighbor in need, pick up litter, do volunteer work, plant a garden, and so on.) Solicit students' ideas for an improvement or beautification project they can undertake for your school neighborhood. Students can vote for their favorite idea, then work together to develop a plan for implementing the project.

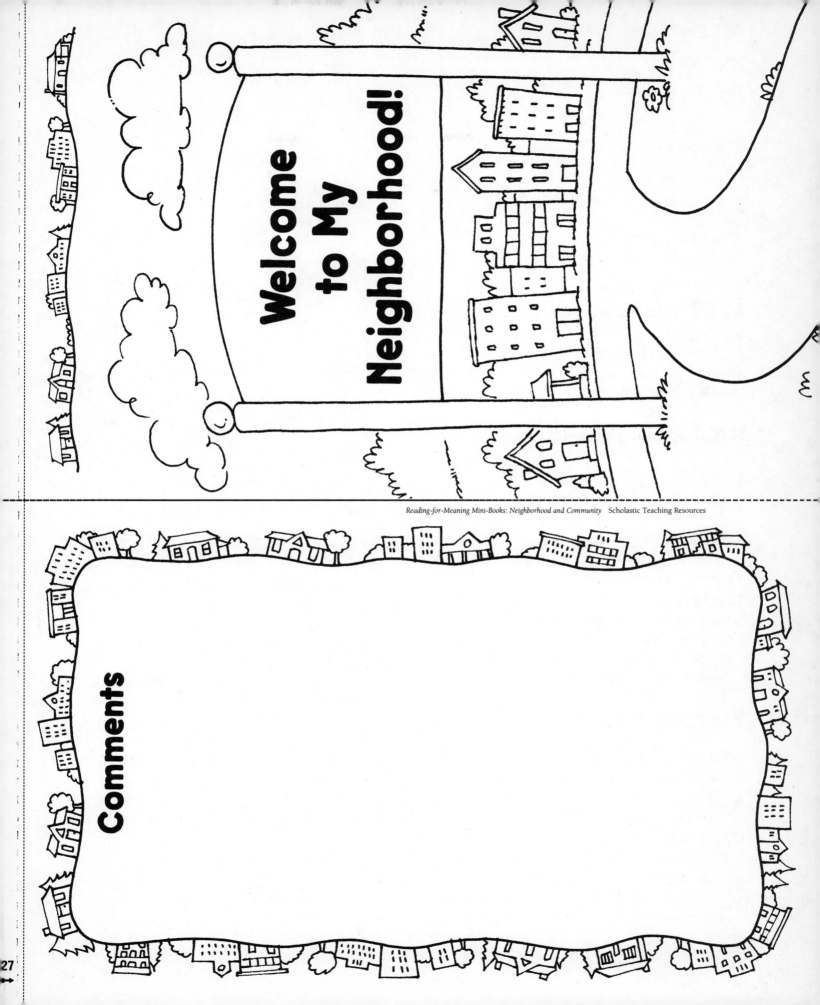

Welcome to My Neighborhood!

Reading-for-Meaning Mini-Books: Neighborhood and Community Scholastic Teaching Resources

Comments

This is where I play.

2

Reading-for-Meaning Mini-Books: Neighborhood and Community Scholastic Teaching Resources

This is where I live.

1

These are a few
of the neighbors I know.

4

Reading-for-Meaning Mini-Books: Neighborhood and Community   Scholastic Teaching Resources

These are some things
that I see every day.

3

The thing I like best about my

neighborhood is _____

_____

_____

_____

_____

_____

_____

I like my neighborhood.
I think you would, too.
Come visit sometime
and I'll show it to you!

6

Reading-for-Meaning Mini-Books: Neighborhood and Community   Scholastic Teaching Resources

This is a place that I like to go.

5

I Like Living in the City

Reading-for-Meaning Mini-Books: Neighborhood and Community   Scholastic Teaching Resources

Comments

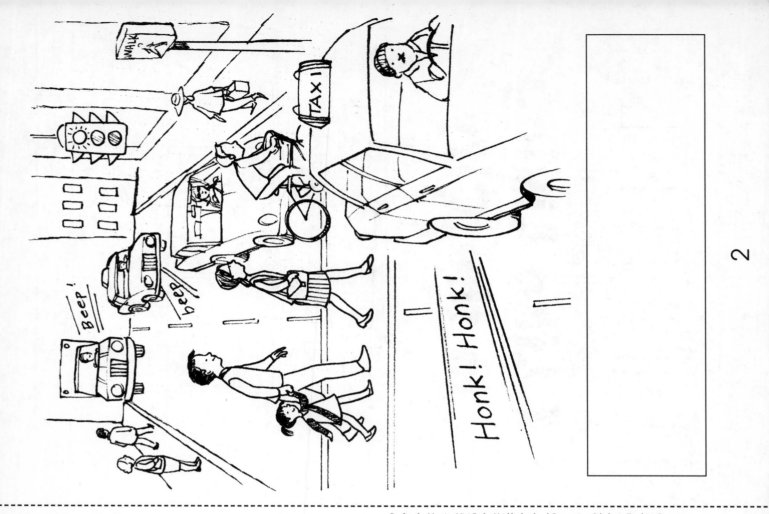

Reading-for-Meaning Mini-Books: Neighborhood and Community Scholastic Teaching Resources

I like living in the city.

4

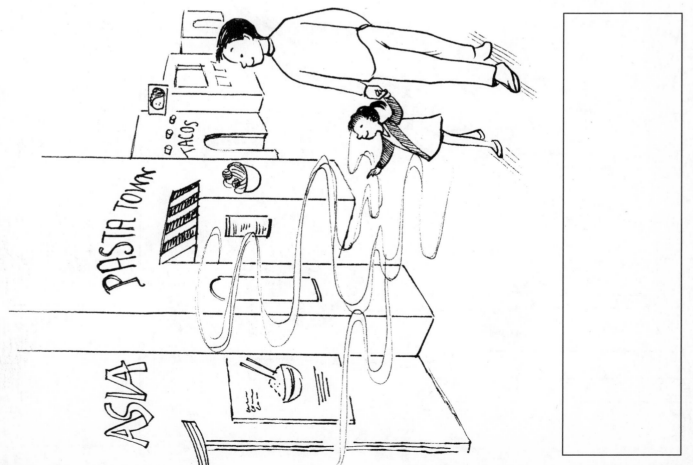

3

I like living in the city.
There's nowhere else I'd rather be!

6

Reading-for-Meaning Mini-Books: Neighborhood and Community Scholastic Teaching Resources

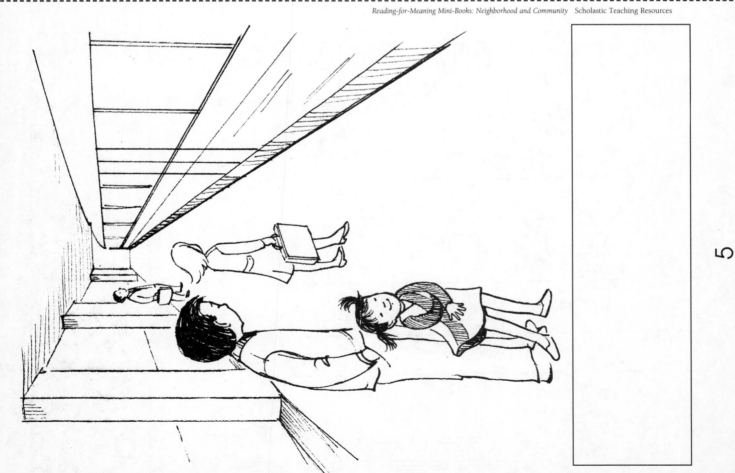

5

I Like Living in the Country

Reading-for-Meaning Mini-Books: Neighborhood and Community Scholastic Teaching Resources

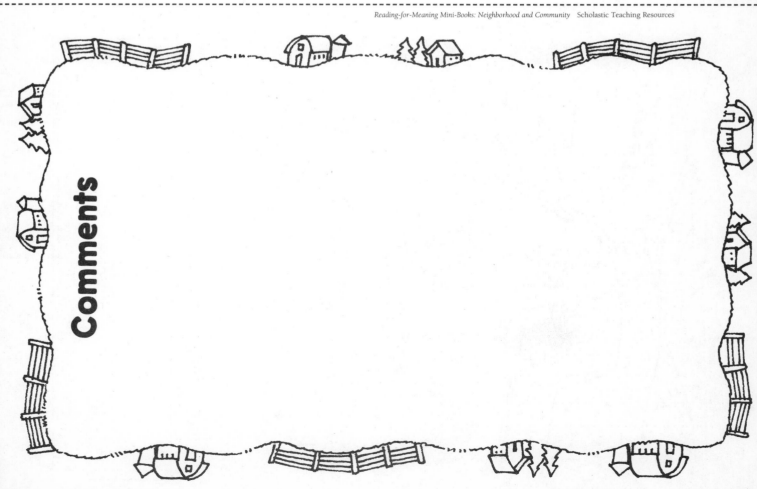

Comments

clippity clop

clippity clop

2

Reading-for-Meaning Mini-Books: Neighborhood and Community   Scholastic Teaching Resources

I like living in the country.

1

3

4

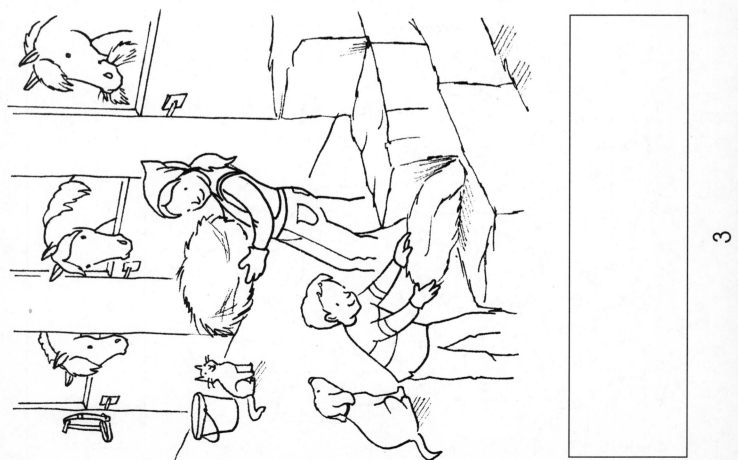

3

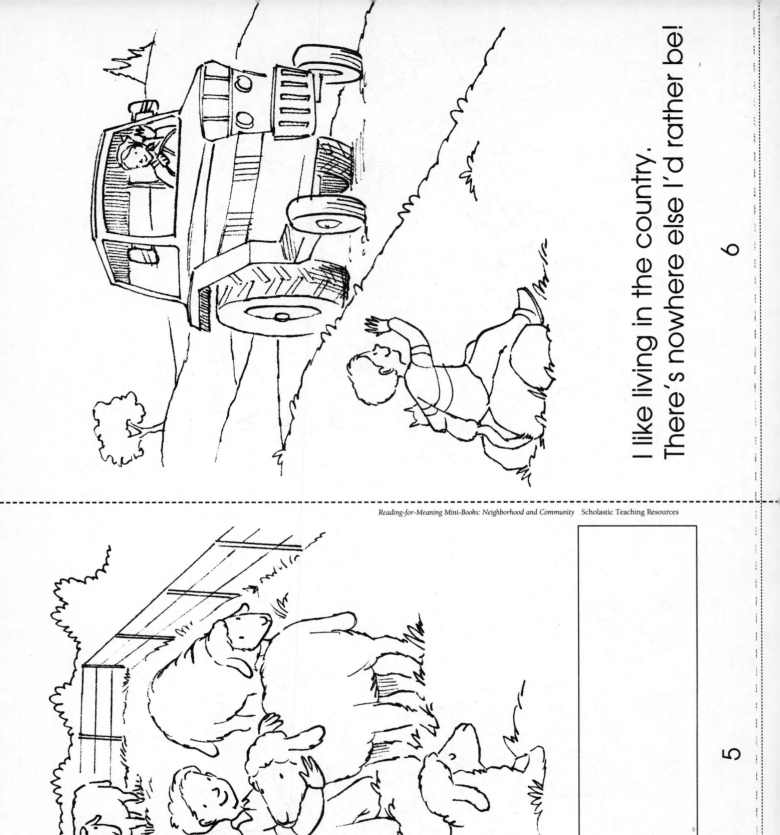

I like living in the country.
There's nowhere else I'd rather be!

6

Reading-for-Meaning Mini-Books: Neighborhood and Community Scholastic Teaching Resources

5

I like to see the tall buildings that touch the sky.

I like the fresh smell of hay that's just been cut.

I like the yummy smells coming from all the different restaurants.

I like to feel the rush of air on my skin when a train goes thundering by.

I like to hear the sound of horses galloping through the pasture.

I like the tickly feel of a sheep's wooly coat.

I like to see the rolling green fields that stretch for miles.

I like to hear the noisy music of cars and taxis honking down the streets.

I like to taste the sweet, crisp apples from our neighbor's orchard.

I like to taste the salty pretzels that vendors sell on every corner.

Reading-for-Meaning Mini-Books: Neighborhood and Community Scholastic Teaching Resources

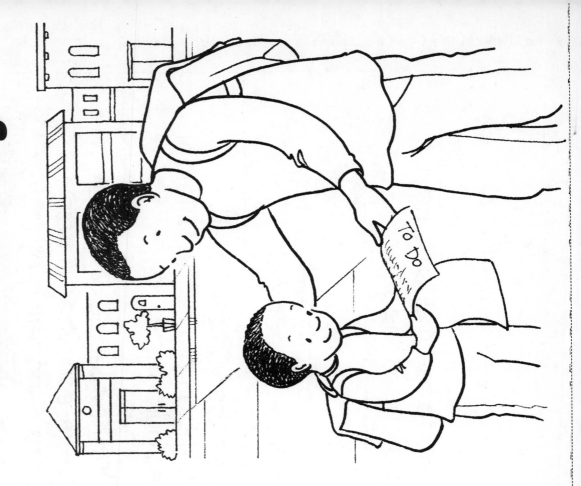

Busy, Busy Saturday

Reading-for-Meaning Mini-Books: Neighborhood and Community   Scholastic Teaching Resources

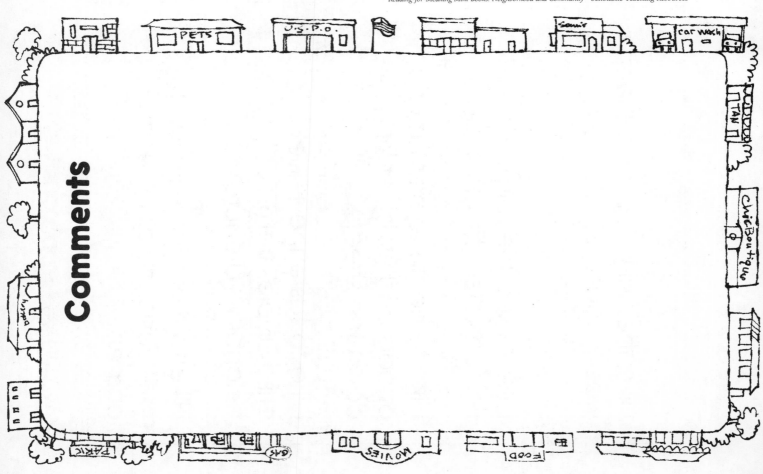

Comments

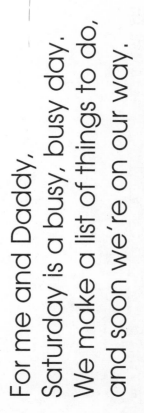

We need to wash our clothes.
We go to the _____.

2

Reading-for-Meaning Mini-Books: Neighborhood and Community   Scholastic Teaching Resources

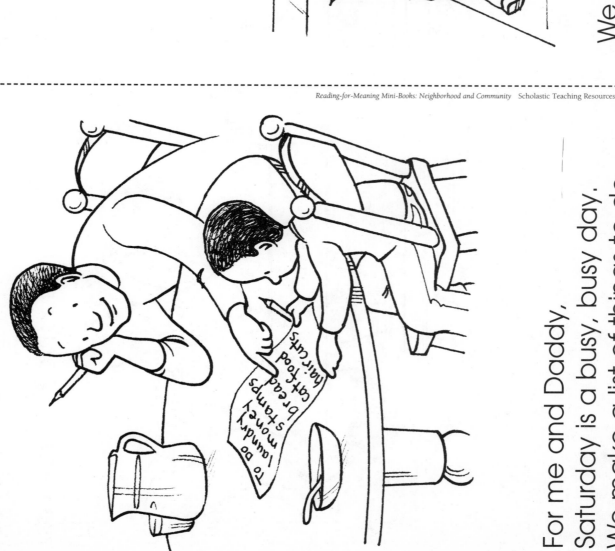

For me and Daddy,
Saturday is a busy, busy day.
We make a list of things to do,
and soon we're on our way.

1

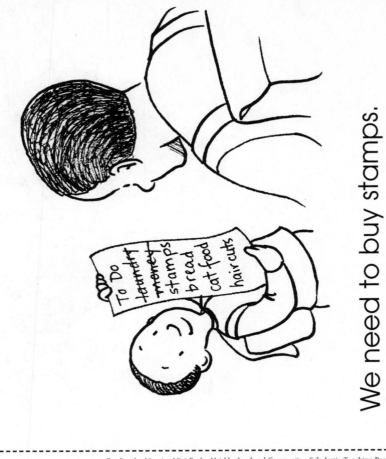

We need to buy stamps.

We go to the _____.

Reading-for-Meaning Mini-Books: Neighborhood and Community Scholastic Teaching Resources

We need to get money.

We go to the _____.

We need to buy cat food.

We go to the _____.

6

We need to buy bread.

We go to the _____.

5

We finished all our errands.
What a busy day!
Now Daddy and I
are ready for fun,
so we go to the _____

to play.

8

Reading-for-Meaning Mini-Books: Neighborhood and Community   Scholastic Teaching Resources

We need to get our hair cut.
We go to the _____.

7

The Library

Reading-for-Meaning Mini-Books: Neighborhood and Community Scholastic Teaching Resources

Comments

The librarian helps me find books and checks them out for me.

2

Reading-for-Meaning Mini-Books: Neighborhood and Community Scholastic Teaching Resources

In my town, there is a library. It's my favorite place to be.

1

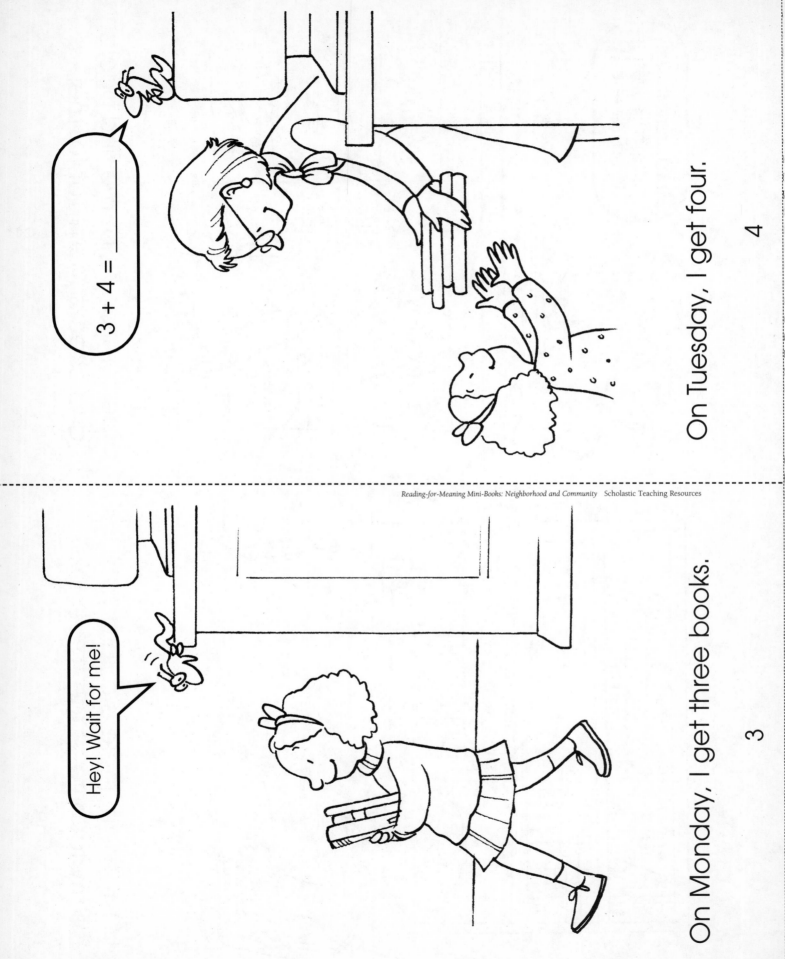

On Tuesday, I get four.

4

On Monday, I get three books.

3

12 + 2 = _____

On Thursday, I get two more.

6

Reading-for-Meaning Mini-Books: Neighborhood and Community   Scholastic Teaching Resources

7 + 5 = _____

On Wednesday, I get five books.

5

On Saturday, I just stay home
and read and read and read!

8

Reading-for-Meaning Mini-Books: Neighborhood and Community   Scholastic Teaching Resources

On Friday, I get six books.
I think that's all I need.

7

Who Helps?

Reading-for-Meaning Mini-Books: Neighborhood and Community Scholastic Teaching Resources

Comments

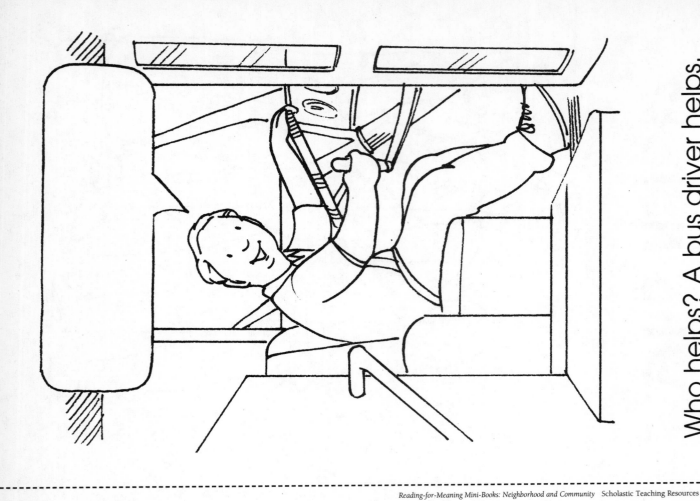

Who helps? A bus driver helps.

2

Reading-for-Meaning Mini-Books: Neighborhood and Community   Scholastic Teaching Resources

DON'T
Talk to Strangers

Who helps? A police officer helps.

1

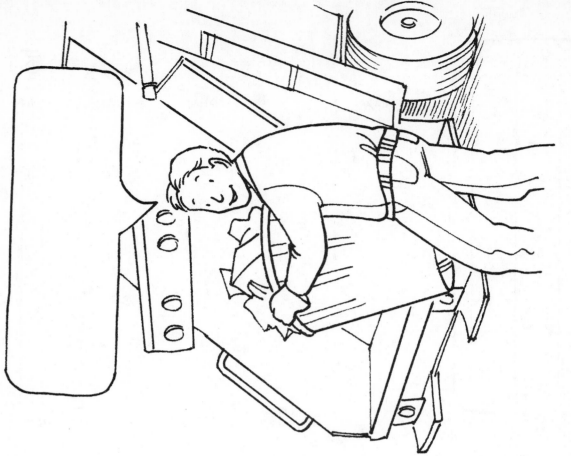

Who helps?
A garbage collector helps.

4

Reading-for-Meaning Mini-Books: Neighborhood and Community Scholastic Teaching Resources

Who helps? A dentist helps.

3

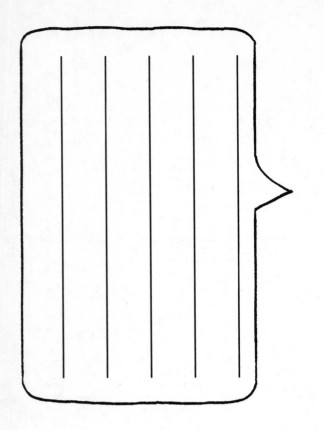

Who helps?

A _____ helps.

6

Reading-for-Meaning Mini-Books: Neighborhood and Community   Scholastic Teaching Resources

Who helps? A mechanic helps.

5

I help you get from
place to place.

I help fix cars
that are broken.

I help keep your
neighborhood clean.

I help keep you and
your neighborhood safe.

I help keep your
teeth healthy.

Reading-for-Meaning Mini-Books: Neighborhood and Community Scholastic Teaching Resources

Here Come the Firefighters!

Reading-for-Meaning Mini-Books: Neighborhood and Community Scholastic Teaching Resources

Comments

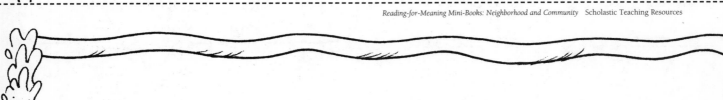

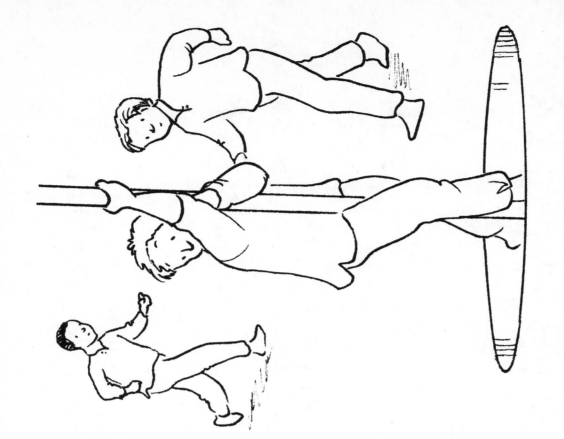

Slide down the pole
as the bell starts to ring.

Reading-for-Meaning Mini-Books: Neighborhood and Community   Scholastic Teaching Resources

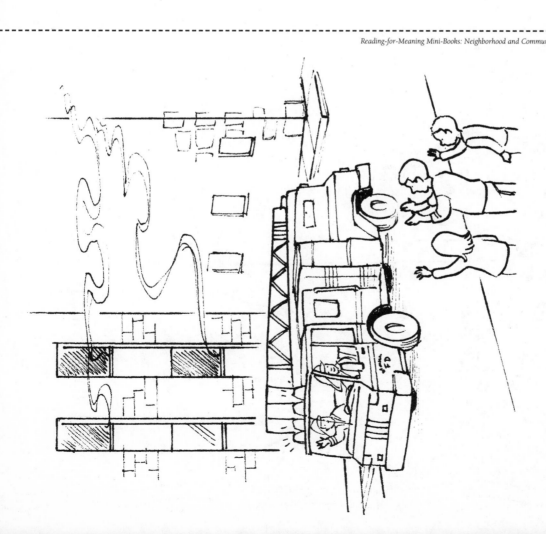

Everyone is safe
and the fire is out!
"Hooray for the firefighters!"
the people all shout.

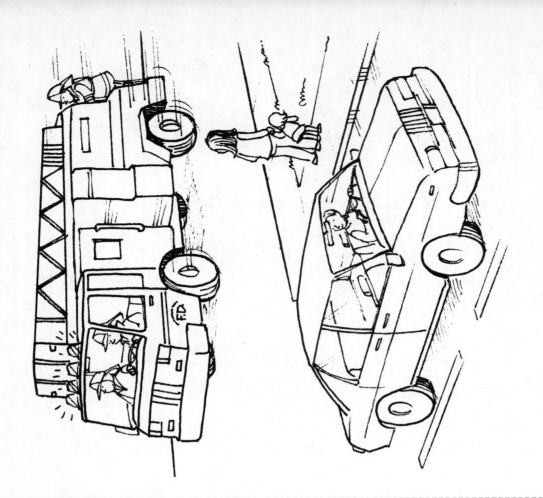

Climb in the truck.
Zoom down the street.

Reading-for-Meaning Mini-Books: Neighborhood and Community   Scholastic Teaching Resources

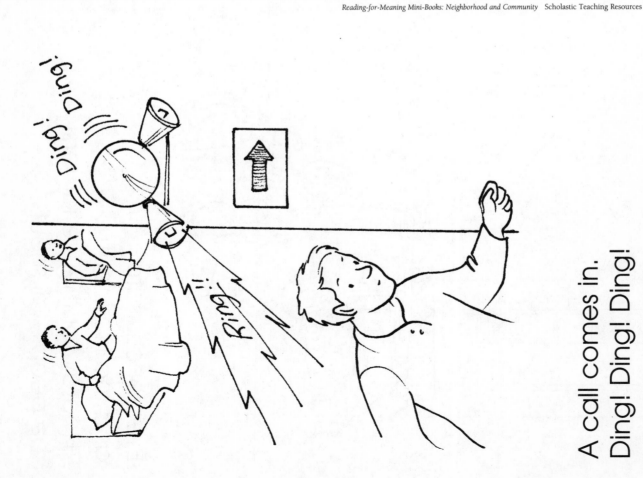

A call comes in.
Ding! Ding! Ding!

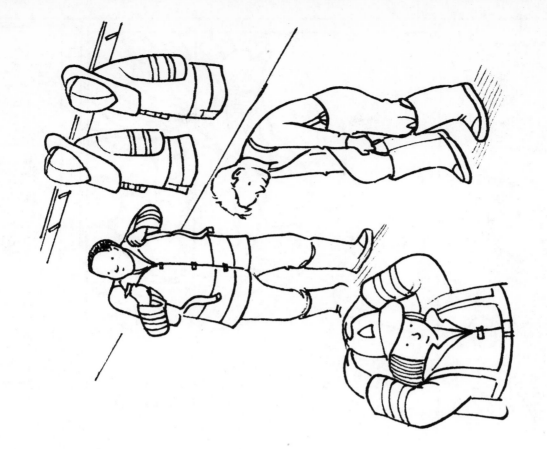

Put your helmet on your head and boots on your feet.

Reading-for-Meaning Mini-Books: Neighborhood and Community Scholastic Teaching Resources

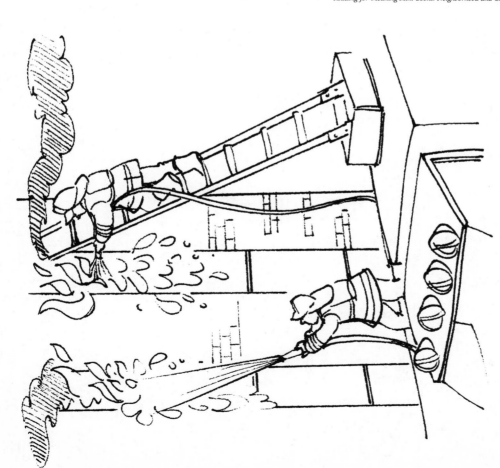

Raise the ladder, higher, higher, higher!
Aim the hoses at the fire.

The Mango Man

Bananas 35¢ each

Apples 40¢ each

Oranges 50¢ each

Fresh FRUIT

Reading-for-Meaning Mini-Books: Neighborhood and Community Scholastic Teaching Resources

Comments

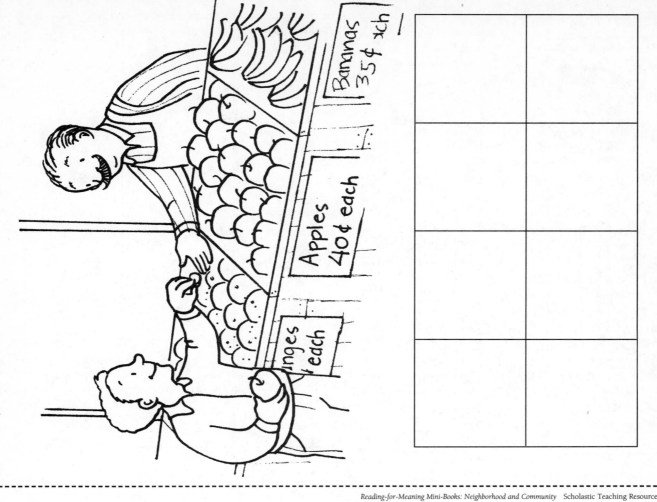

He sells an apple to Mr. Alvarez.

2

Reading-for-Meaning Mini-Books: Neighborhood and Community   Scholastic Teaching Resources

The Mango Man sells fruit to everyone in town.

1

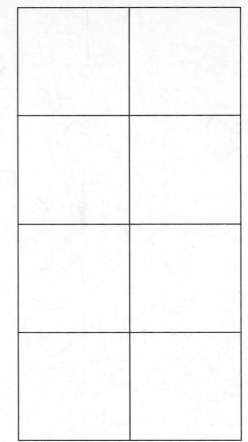

He sells a pound of grapes
to Ms. Silverman.

4

Reading-for-Meaning Mini-Books: Neighborhood and Community   Scholastic Teaching Resources

a banana to Mrs. Brown.

3

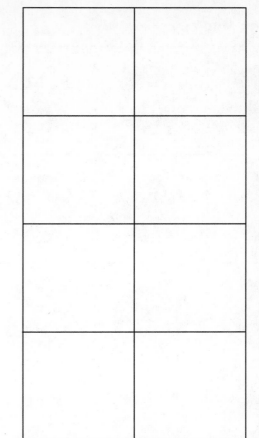

And every day the Mango Man
saves a mango just for me!

6

Reading-for-Meaning Mini-Books: Neighborhood and Community   Scholastic Teaching Resources

an orange to Mr. Lee.

5

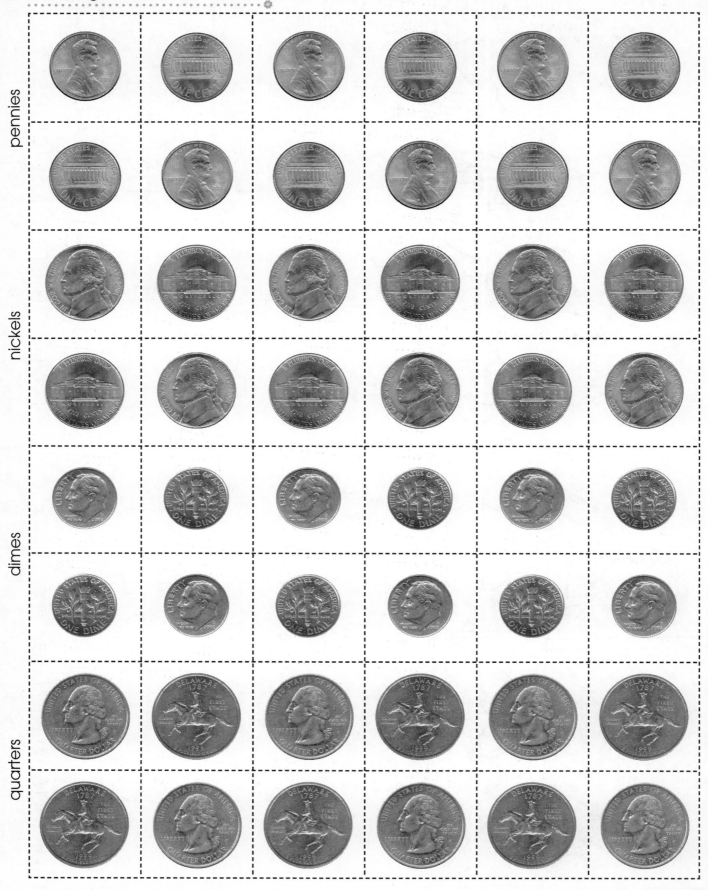

pennies

nickels

dimes

quarters

Reading-for-Meaning Mini-Books: Neighborhood and Community Scholastic Teaching Resources

The Mail Carrier

Reading-for-Meaning Mini-Books: Neighborhood and Community   Scholastic Teaching Resources

Comments

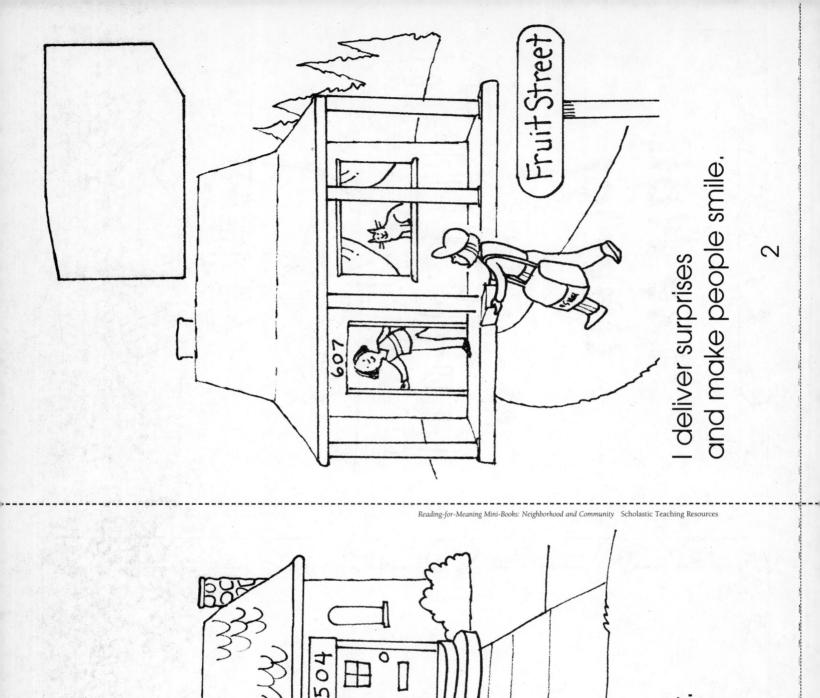

I deliver surprises
and make people smile.

2

Reading-for-Meaning Mini-Books: Neighborhood and Community   Scholastic Teaching Resources

Hi! I am a mail carrier.
I walk mile after mile.

1

I bring packages and postcards from people far away.

4

Reading-for-Meaning Mini-Books: Neighborhood and Community Scholastic Teaching Resources

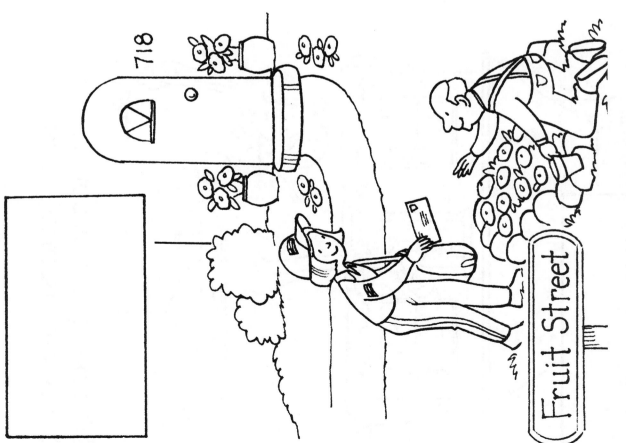

I deliver cards and letters to people every day.

3

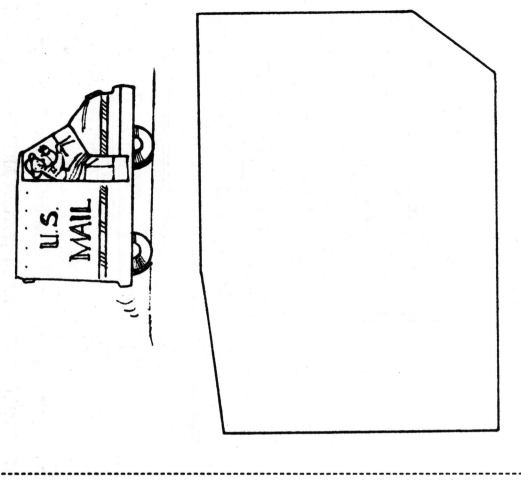

Maybe one day soon I'll bring
a surprise addressed to you!

6

Reading-for-Meaning Mini-Books: Neighborhood and Community Scholastic Teaching Resources

I like being a mail carrier.
It's an important job to do.

5

Mr. Freddy Spaghetti
716 Pasta Place
Sillyville, Kansas
10203

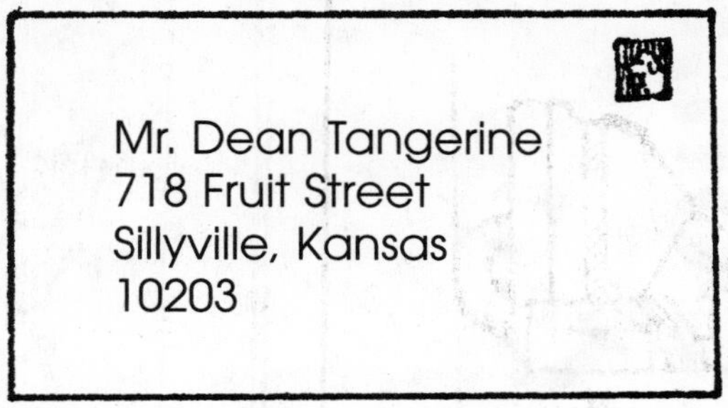

Mr. Dean Tangerine
718 Fruit Street
Sillyville, Kansas
10203

Ms. Hannah Banana
504 Fruit Street
Sillyville, Kansas
10203

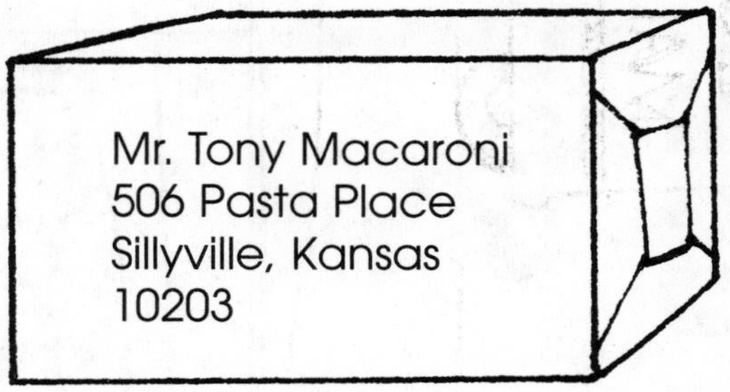

Mr. Tony Macaroni
506 Pasta Place
Sillyville, Kansas
10203

Mrs. Claire Pear
607 Fruit Street
Sillyville, Kansas
10203

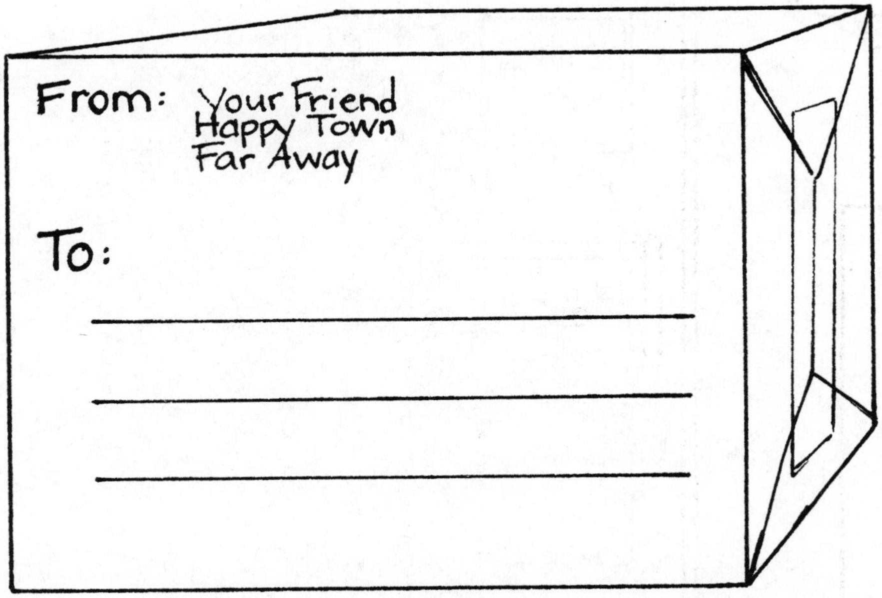

From: Your Friend
Happy Town
Far Away

To:

_____

_____

_____

Reading-for-Meaning Mini-Books: Neighborhood and Community Scholastic Teaching Resources

Trucks Come and Go

Reading-for-Meaning Mini-Books: Neighborhood and Community   Scholastic Teaching Resources

Comments

Some trucks move cars.

2

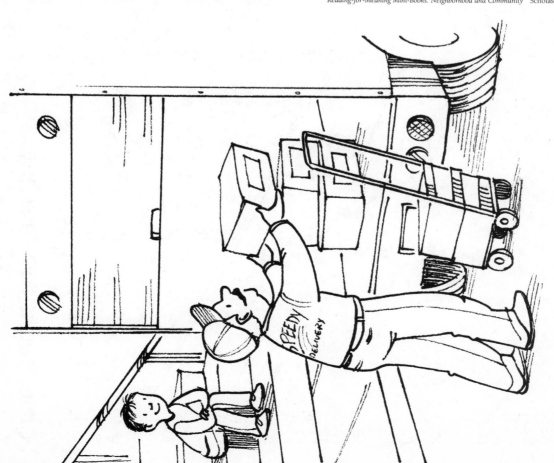

In my neighborhood,
trucks come and go.

1

Some trucks mix cement.

4

Some trucks move snow.

3

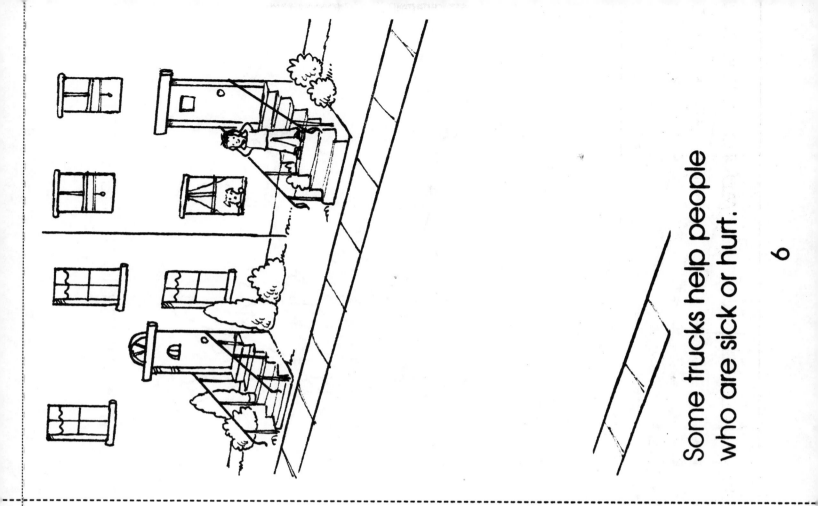

Some trucks help people
who are sick or hurt.

6

Some trucks dig dirt.

5

Some trucks clean the street.

8

Reading-for-Meaning Mini-Books: Neighborhood and Community   Scholastic Teaching Resources

Some trucks move furniture.

7

brings a sweet treat to eat!

10

Reading-for-Meaning Mini-Books: Neighborhood and Community   Scholastic Teaching Resources

But my favorite truck of all

9

ice-cream truck

tow truck

back hoe

moving van

snow plow

street sweeper

ambulance

cement mixer

Reading-for-Meaning Mini-Books: Neighborhood and Community   Scholastic Teaching Resources

Lost!

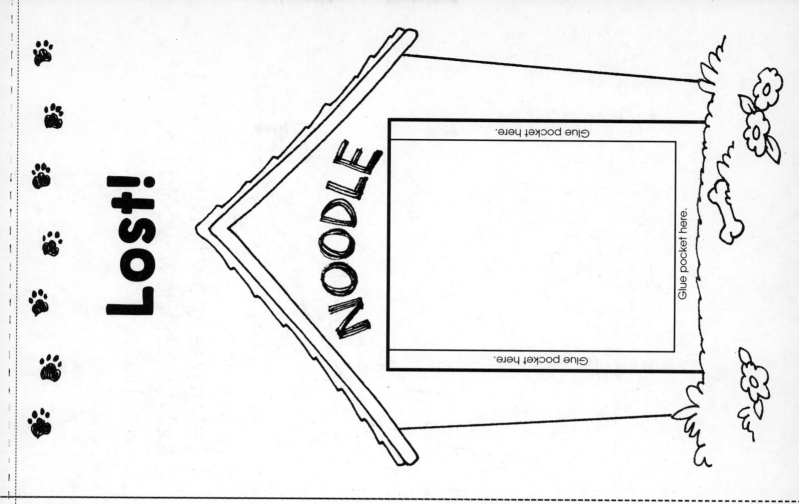

NOODLE

Glue pocket here.

Glue pocket here.

Glue pocket here.

Reading-for-Meaning Mini-Books: Neighborhood and Community   Scholastic Teaching Resources

Comments

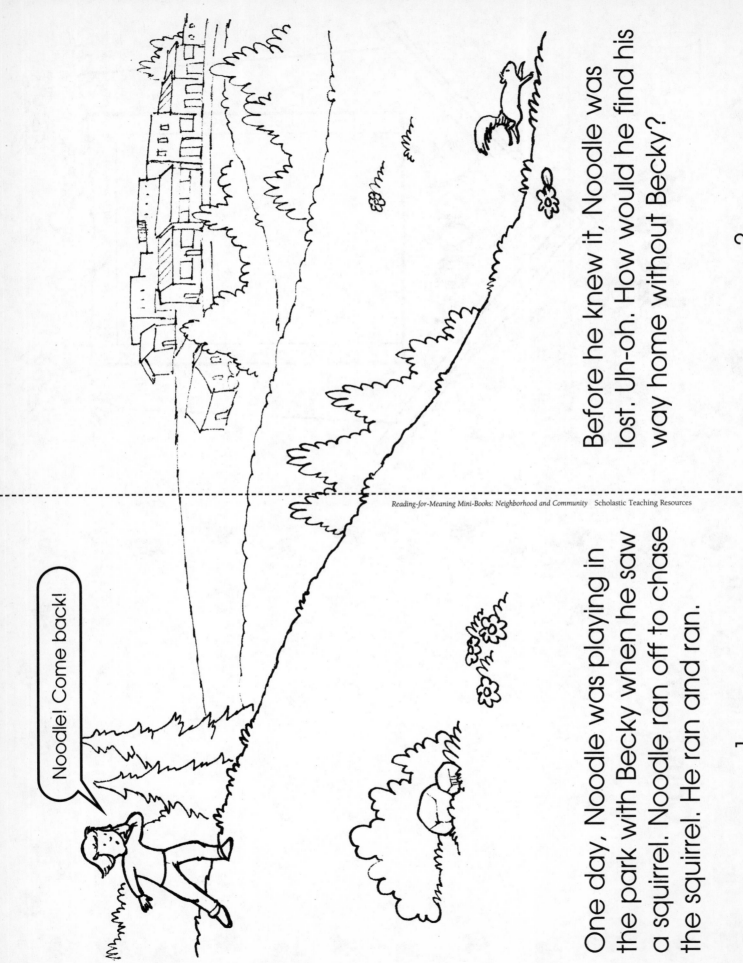

Before he knew it, Noodle was lost. Uh-oh. How would he find his way home without Becky?

2

Reading-for-Meaning Mini-Books: Neighborhood and Community Scholastic Teaching Resources

Noodle! Come back!

One day, Noodle was playing in the park with Becky when he saw a squirrel. Noodle ran off to chase the squirrel. He ran and ran.

1

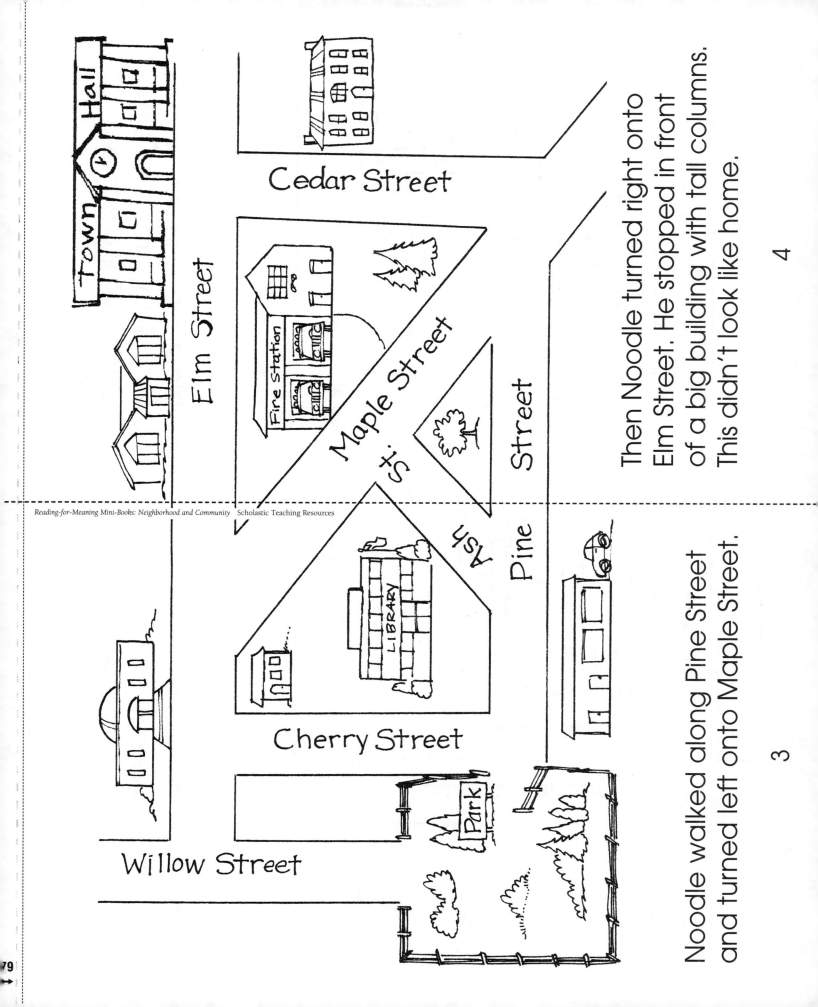

Town Hall

Cedar Street

Elm Street

Maple Street

Fire Station

Ash St.

Pine Street

Library

Cherry Street

Willow Street

Park

Then Noodle turned right onto Elm Street. He stopped in front of a big building with tall columns. This didn't look like home.

4

Noodle walked along Pine Street and turned left onto Maple Street.

3

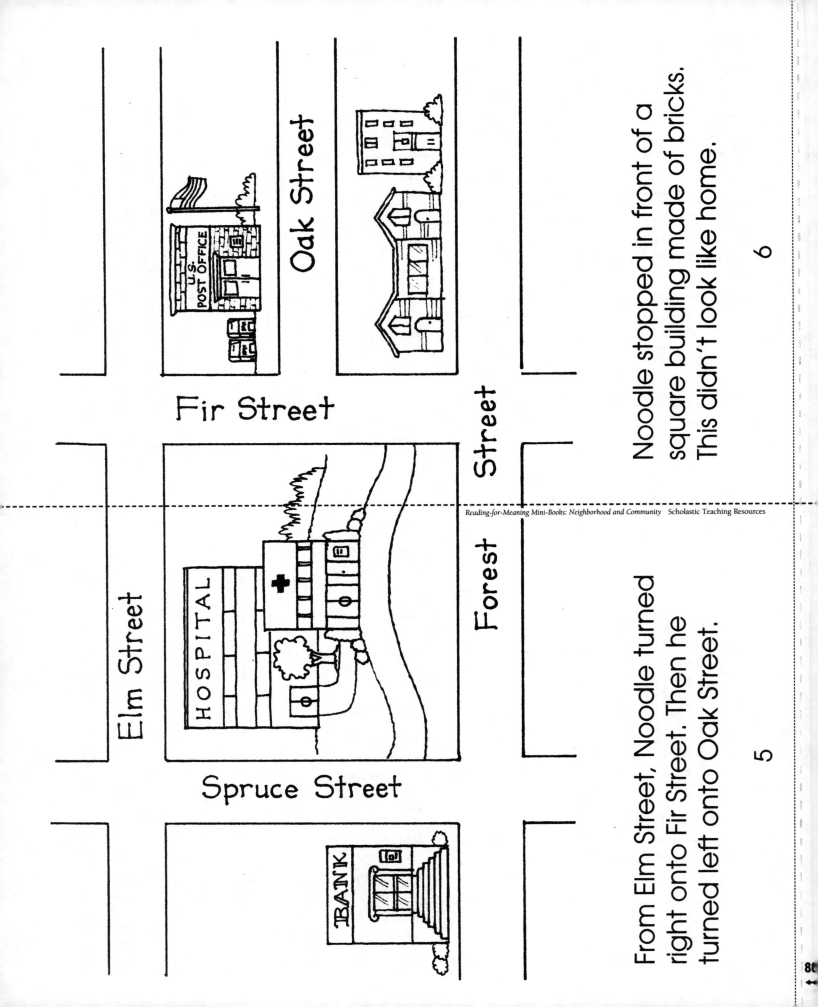

Fir Street

Oak Street

Elm Street

Spruce Street

Forest Street

U.S. POST OFFICE

HOSPITAL

BANK

Noodle stopped in front of a square building made of bricks. This didn't look like home.

6

From Elm Street, Noodle turned right onto Fir Street. Then he turned left onto Oak Street.

5

Reading-for-Meaning Mini-Books: Neighborhood and Community   Scholastic Teaching Resources

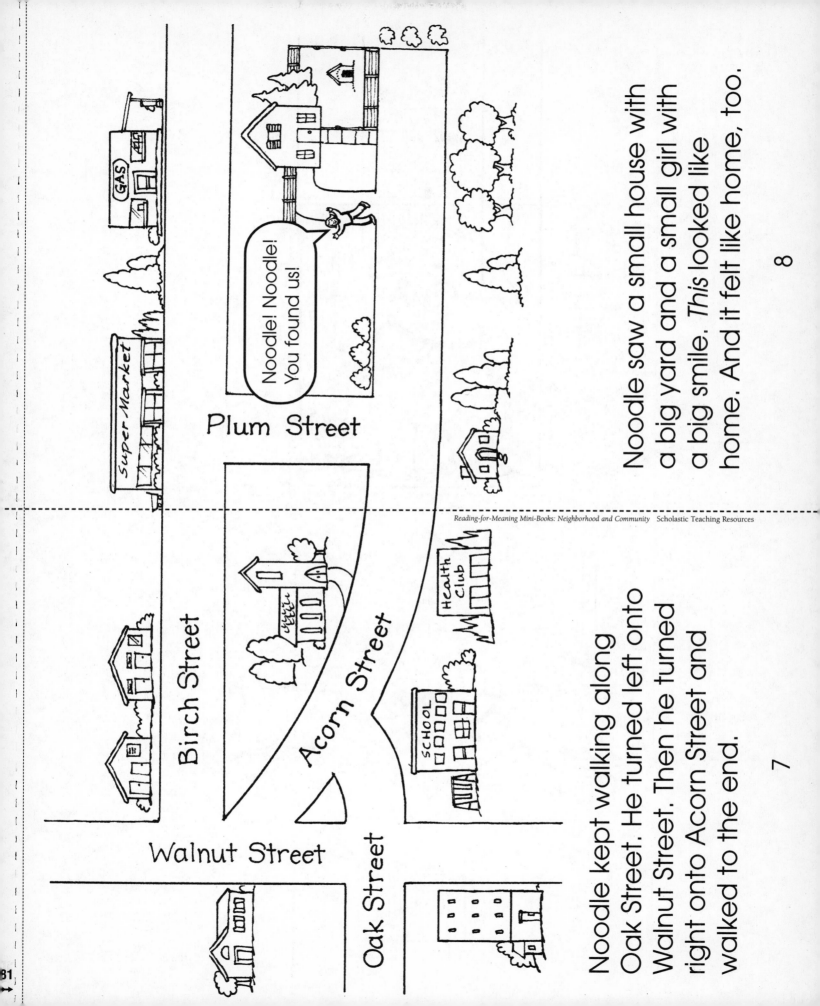

GAS

Super Market

Noodle! Noodle! You found us!

Plum Street

Birch Street

Acorn Street

Walnut Street

Health Club

SCHOOL

Oak Street

Reading-for-Meaning Mini-Books: Neighborhood and Community   Scholastic Teaching Resources

Noodle saw a small house with a big yard and a small girl with a big smile. *This looked like home. And it felt like home, too.*

8

Noodle kept walking along Oak Street. He turned left onto Walnut Street. Then he turned right onto Acorn Street and walked to the end.

7

pattern A

pattern B

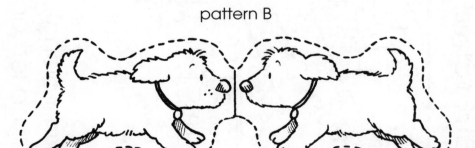

Dream Neighborhood

Reading-for-Meaning Mini-Books: Neighborhood and Community Scholastic Teaching Resources

Comments

I'd like to live in a neighborhood where everyone rides scooters instead of driving cars.

2

Reading-for-Meaning Mini-Books: Neighborhood and Community Scholastic Teaching Resources

I'd like to live in a neighborhood where the houses are shaped like stars.

1

84

I'd like to live in a neighborhood where all the stores are toy stores, and trees grow candy canes to eat.

4

Reading-for-Meaning Mini-Books: Neighborhood and Community   Scholastic Teaching Resources

I'd like to live in a neighborhood where there's a roller coaster on each street.

3

I would/would not like to live in
this neighborhood because

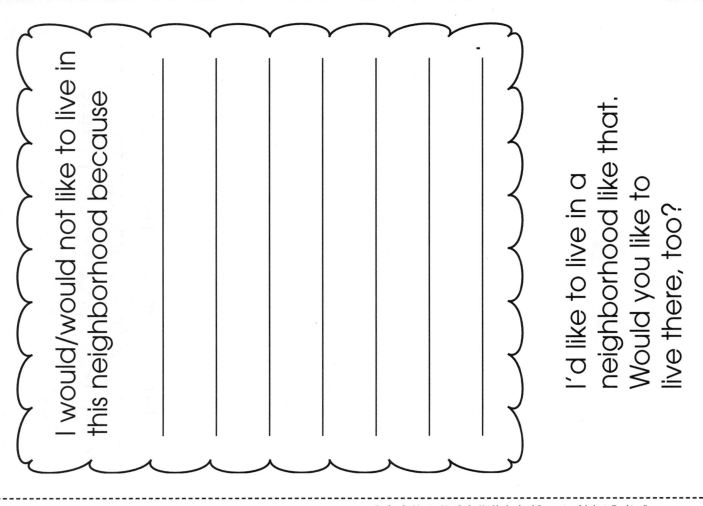

I'd like to live in a
neighborhood like that.
Would you like to
live there, too?

6

Reading-for-Meaning Mini-Books: Neighborhood and Community   Scholastic Teaching Resources

I'd like to live in a neighborhood
where the school has its own zoo.

5

Notes

Notes